D0378398

# WHEN THE
# WORLD BREAKS
# YOUR HEART

# WHEN THE
# WORLD BREAKS
# YOUR HEART

*Spiritual Ways of*
*Living with Tragedy*

GREGORY S. CLAPPER

UPPER
ROOM BOOKS
NASHVILLE

No part of this book may be used or reproduced in any manner whatsoever without written permission of the publisher except in the case of brief quotations embodied in critical articles or reviews. For information, write The Upper Room, P.O. Box 189, Nashville, Tennessee 37202-0189.

Upper Room Web address: http://www.upperroom.org

Scripture quotations not otherwise identified are from the New Revised Standard Version of the Bible, copyright © 1989 by the Division of Christian Education, National Council of the Churches of Christ in the United States of America. Used by permission.

Scripture quotations designated NIV are from the Holy Bible: New International Version. Copyright © 1973, 1978, 1984 International Bible Society. Used by permission of Zondervan Bible Publishers.

Cover design: Gore Studio, Inc.
First printing: 1999

*Library of Congress Cataloging-in-Publication Data*
Clapper, Gregory Scott.
     When the world breaks your heart: spiritual ways to live with tragedy / Gregory S. Clapper.
          p.     cm.
     ISBN 0-8358-0842-4
     1. Consolation.    2. Suffering—Religious aspects—Christianity.
3. Aircraft accidents—Iowa—Sioux City—History. 4. Clapper, Gregory Scott.   I. Title.
BV4905.2.C53     1999
248.8'6--dc21                                                98-19154
                                                                  CIP

Printed in the United States of America

*To my parents,*
*and to those who died, suffered, and served in the crash*
*of United Airlines Flight 232 and its aftermath*

# · CONTENTS ·

· ACKNOWLEDGMENTS ·

To the many people who read this manuscript and helped to shape it, I am deeply indebted. First and foremost is my wife, Jody, who helped me first get through deep tragedy and then supported my writing about it. Jeanie Hall, the world's greatest church secretary, typed many pages of this book from dictation tapes and was patient and helpful throughout the process. Judy Ebert assisted Jeanie. Friends who read through various versions of this manuscript and shared their heartfelt responses include Pastor Larry Keene, Rev. Kathy Leithner, Suzanne Yates, Carl Dillon, Alice Kruse, Marty Van Hemert, Teresa Dickmann, Susan Callender, Rebecca Laird Christensen, Chaplain Kathy Schindel, Col. Dennis Swanstrom, Rev. Wayne Clark, Leasha Schemmel, Lt. Col. James Lundy, and Helen Amos. To those who have shared their friendship with me, and in doing so, shared God's grace with me, I am especially indebted. Among these are Clayton Kooiker, Elmer Sale, Goose Tatum, and Kate and Dan Lindsey.

This book is written to help people cope with the mystery of tragedy, whether it be a tragedy in their own lives or a tragedy in the life of a friend. I share six spiritual resources that I know can make a difference in the aftermath of a tragedy. Some of these resources, like the concept of mystery itself that I address in the first chapter, are informed by my training as a theologian and my work as a professor. Others, like the chapters on tears and the presence of God, are more directly informed by my personal experience as a minister, a chaplain, and simply as a Christian.

All six chapters, though, are illustrated by reference to my work as a chaplain after the crash of United Airlines Flight 232 in Sioux City, Iowa, on July 19, 1989. As a result of that crash 183 people survived and 113 died. My purpose is not to try to tell all of the important stories of the crash and rescue effort, but rather to show how six resources from the Christian tradition—mystery, tears, humility, gentleness, hope, and the presence of God— helped to draw people, including me, into new life after a real-life tragedy.

One of the truths that I came to appreciate during my ministry after the plane crash is that our personal histories are the lenses that bring the present into focus. Only in, with, and through our personal histories can we deal with the reality of tragedy. Because of this, in writing about tragedy I have spoken freely about my own personal history. Dispassionate, and impersonal approaches to this topic seem both irrelevant and inappropriate.

I have provided questions for reflection at the end of each chapter. These are not abstract or academic questions but questions designed to help the reader deal with tragedy in the context of his or her own spiritual life. You may find it profitable to write your responses to these questions. Writing your spiritual reflections and raising your own questions—sometimes called *journaling*—is a long-honored practice in the Christian tradition. Whether or not you respond in writing, though, you may find that one or more of the questions is simply worth living with for a while. Sometimes the questions we ask form us more than the answers we believe we are looking for. If our hearts are in the asking, God will meet us in these questions and sustain us in this strange and powerful process of soul-formation called the Christian journey.

# THE MYSTERY OF TRAGEDY

O
n that hot July afternoon when United Airlines
Flight 232 crashed, my family and I were driving
into Sioux City from our home in Le Mars to see
the movie *Peter Pan*. A nostalgic reverie about the television movie *Peter Pan*, with Mary Martin flying around
the stage on wires we could see but chose to ignore, con-
sumed me. The song "I Can Fly" was certainly a kind of
theme song for youth, a celebration of the unfettered
imagination and unlimited possibilities of childhood.

As we pulled into the Southern Hills Mall, I noticed a
plane flying low heading for the nearby airport. Just as we
pulled into a space in the mall parking lot, we saw a thick
line of black smoke rise from the direction of the airport.
As my family got out of the car, I sat in the car, put the
key back in the ignition, and turned on the radio, await-
ing word in case the worst imaginable thing had actually

happened. Immediately the radio announcer said there was an unconfirmed report of a plane crash at the Sioux Gateway Airport.

As soon as I heard that, I felt a crushing sensation in my chest. It was as though that news report suddenly squeezed out of me the plans I had made for that afternoon—and for the rest of my life. Instead of celebrating a flight of imagination in a cool theater, I would face a blunt reality on a hot runway. Instead of relishing the limitless possibilities of youth, I would have to deal with the limited options that tragedy presents to us.

I started the car, told my family to get back in, and we drove the few minutes distance to the airport. Even with that short time between the crash and my arrival, already a long string of cars lined the shoulder of the interstate, the drivers curious to watch what was happening at the airport. When I got to the airport exit, a state trooper was waving everyone on, not allowing anyone to exit. I pulled over and showed him my identification indicating that I was a member of the Air National Guard. I told the officer, "I am a chaplain and need to be at the crash scene." He said, "Mister, I don't care. No one is getting off here." I pulled off about a hundred feet past the exit from I-29 and got out. I told my wife, Jody, that I would somehow get my own ride back home. As she drove off with our two daughters, I started running toward the entrance to the runway.

After my initial ministry with the injured and those still trapped in the wreckage—which I will speak more about later—I turned my attention to the uninjured survivors. Rescue workers carried these people from the runway to the headquarters building on our Air Guard base so that they would not clog up the hospitals and possibly prevent care from being given to the more seriously hurt. When I got to the headquarters building, survivors filled the dining hall. People sat everywhere, some on chairs, some on blankets. As I started circulating among the survivors, a worker directed me to two small children.

These two children, a brother and sister no more than six or eight years of age, had been traveling with their mother in the plane. Their mother now lay dead on the runway. The little girl, Rachel, and her brother, Peter (not their real names), sat quietly without emotion—no crying, no hysteria. They seemed subdued. I sat down to talk to them, and Rachel perked up a little when I noticed the teddy bear earring in one of her ears, and she gladly showed me both, obviously proud of these special gifts. I asked, "Is there anything I can do for you?" They said, "No." Running out of all other alternatives, I asked if they needed to go to the bathroom and Peter said "Yes." I took him down the hall to the men's room. After relieving ourselves, we washed our hands in the same sink. I noticed that I had some blood on my hands, and it went down the drain with the dirt from Peter's hands. We went back to the dining hall, and Peter rejoined his sister on the floor, in silence. Their shocked, silent numbness will forever be for me a symbol of our human response to mystery.

## The Reality of Mystery

The popular books and movies that go by the name "mystery" do not best exemplify true mystery. These "mysteries" are more like puzzles that will yield their answers to the clever. A true mystery, though, in the classical theological sense of that term, is not something that the clever person will solve before the dullard. A true mystery is one that will not yield to *any* explanation. There are some questions that will never receive satisfying answers. Such mysteries bring us to our knees, literally and spiritually. One of the reasons the classical understanding of mystery has become clouded is that there are many persons in academia—that place where we go to learn about life—who do not consciously recognize the reality of mysteries.

Academia, where I was spending my professional energy at the time of the crash, is not a place that breeds humility. Quite often, recipients of the Ph.D. degree see it as granting comprehensive authority, a kind of license for pride. It is, of course, possible for people to inhabit the "ivory tower" with integrity if they do not forget the mud and muck that they left behind them. All too often, though, competitiveness for good professional positions and the gamesmanship of applying for promotions and grant money, squeeze true mystery out of the picture. Academics tend to approach any subject as a problem that will yield its solution to just the right scholar armed with the proper credentials, a sabbatical, and research funding.

But whether or not academia wants to recognize it, all of humanity is in fact thrust into the middle of huge mysteries, and the mystery of tragedy is perhaps the deepest of them all. Tragedy comes into our lives in many ways, such as the death of a loved one, crippling and terminal diseases, rape, abuse, floods, hurricanes, fires, earthquakes, auto accidents, or plane crashes. The outward circumstances of tragedy can be widely different. All tragedies, however, have at least one thing in common. This element shared by all tragedies is a strong sense that such an event should not have happened.

In a tragedy, we think that somehow, somewhere, something went wrong, a mistake has been made. Whether it is on a microscopic level (as in cancer), a mechanical level (such as when a failing part causes a crash), a willful, human level (when criminal acts are deliberately undertaken), or on a cosmic level (such as when people are killed by a tornado), something has gone terribly wrong. If we call something a tragedy, we think it should not have happened.

When we finally confront the baffling depth and shocking darkness of true mystery, whether our initial reaction is wildly emotional or not, there is a part of all of us that goes numb, a part of us that stares into the abyss and comes away with pupils fixed and dilated. I saw this in the faces of Rachel and Peter, sitting alone among strangers and in the strong absence of their mother. Stunned. Silent. Covered from head to toe with a body stocking of thick emotional goose down, submerged up to the mouth in a vat of thick oil, able to breathe, but not much else.

True mystery shatters the illusion that we have total control over our lives. Things are not as we would have them be and there is no changing that. When we are in the midst of mystery, our mouths are stopped. We have to retreat to the childlike impotence that we were born into. We can behold, but we cannot comprehend.

The encounter with true mystery is not so much a new or radically intense kind of "experience" or "feeling": it is more a lack of feeling or numbness. It is a kind of electroshock therapy where all of the previous signals transmitted by the brain through the nervous system become temporarily jumbled into meaningless static. To try to describe the static is useless, for what has happened is a disruption of the very signal-making process that is necessary to describe anything. All that you are aware of is numbness.

Such numbness does not leave easily. Some of it, perhaps, never goes away. After we find ourselves in a mystery, a part of us will always remember that unmistakable feeling of having a window open in our house that we cannot close, no matter how hard we try. For most of us at least, though, we do not remain forever in that stage of numbness. We start "coming to" and begin the frustrating but necessary task of finding our way around in the mystery that has engulfed us.

## THE MYSTERY OF TRAGEDY

The particular mystery that those recovering from the plane crash had to deal with is the mystery of tragic death. Why did Rachel and Peter's mother die while they survived? The question of why the plane crashed was not a mystery, but merely a problem to be solved by the National Transportation Safety Board (NTSB), the Federal Aviation Administration (FAA), and other agencies. In fact, the answer was quite clear: an engine part disintegrated and severed all of the plane's hydraulic lines. Problem solved. But now the real mystery only looms larger: Why must we live in a world where such things can happen? Why do we live in a world where cancer takes the lives of children? Why do we live in a world where the high school dropout gets drunk and ends up crashing into and killing the class valedictorian? Why does a loving God allow such a world to be?

Why? The FAA, the whole government, even the pooled insight of religious professionals, no one can give an answer that takes away the pain. This is mystery, true mystery. There can be no solutions to mystery, only different ways of dealing with it. After the stunned silence—or after failing to fill up the infinite void of silence with hysteria—we begin to see something. We start to see that we at least have choices about how we describe these mysteries and how we respond to them. Life is, in fact, really a matter in which we "choose our mystery."

## CHOOSE YOUR MYSTERY

When mystery is discussed, some will scoff and turn away. These people, who often think of themselves as "hard-headed realists," avoid religion because religion openly acknowledges—and even proclaims—mysteries, mysteries such as the mystery of the incarnation of God in Christ, the mystery of our salvation purchased by Jesus on the cross, and the mystery of evil. They prefer life "straight," without any "nonsense" about mystery.

The problem with such folks is that they will not acknowledge the mysteries that they themselves live in. A completely secularized person might think that real "honest" life is nothing but seeking pleasure and avoiding pain, but they have often never considered the shape of the mystery of their own reality as they themselves describe it. For instance, "Why is pleasure so fleeting and pain so common? Why are some more able than others to achieve safety, satisfaction, and comfort? If the goal of life is to have a big weekend, why must we slog through the challenges of the work week first?" Since we cannot avoid all mystery, these questions lead to the reality of mystery. They lead us to two bottom-line questions of life: Which mystery will I call my own? How will I deal with it?

When we deal with the mystery of evil, suffering, and tragedy, there are three classic options which offer themselves to us. One option, the one taken by many Eastern religions, is to deny the ultimate reality of suffering, to say that it is an illusion. Most Westerners do not pay much regard to this option. The second option, sometimes cloaked under the name "existentialism," looks at tragedy and says "that is all life is." Those who choose this option adopt either a stoical attitude of courageously facing the apparent meaninglessness of life or else throw themselves into an attempt to forget their plight through work, substance addiction, or perhaps suicide. They have decided that either malevolent or totally indifferent forces guide life. The third option is that seen in the classical Christian understanding of life.

## Christian Responses to Tragedy

The believer, formed in the biblical faith, also experiences—and owns—the numbness and pain of the mystery as well. To pretend otherwise, to deny it, as some misguided Christians do, is nothing but sad folly, and such repression can lead to problems. But the believer, after acknowledging and naming this mystery, is lovingly and patiently called back to trusting that this mystery called life—with all of its emotional blind alleys and spiritual dead ends—is finally a gift, and that the gift is good.

The Christian who has read and understood the book of Job, the Christian who has read the passion narratives of Christ and has understood and embodied them, will know that the faithful one is no stranger to mystery, and specifically to the mystery of tragedy. Tragedy is, in fact, a true mystery *only for those who have a faith that creation does somehow make sense*, those who have a faith in a higher being, those who believe in God.

If you start with the premise that we are all random atoms colliding with each other, then why should anything make any sense? Why should planes not crash, families be torn apart, or children die of cancer? If that were the case, then why should individual life be nothing but mindless self-centeredness and self-absorbed pleasure-seeking, where the stomach and the groin are the true masters? As we unfortunately can see in our culture, many have (consciously or not) opted for this view of life.

Jesus Christ, on the other hand, stood in the midst of the mystery of human life and death and neither repressed this mystery nor pretended to answer it. As seen in Luke 13, where Jesus is asked to "explain" a tragedy, he responds by asking, "Were those who had the temple of Siloam fall on them any worse than anyone else?" He dismisses such hateful speculation about the victims of tragedies by simply saying, "No," and then goes on to call for repentance among all those who hear him. Jesus Christ acknowledged the reality of tragedy and went on with life. Tragedy neither drove him to despair nor did it elicit a long "explanation." Jesus simply lived the mystery of a grace-filled loving life in the midst of tragedy and called his followers to do the same.

Some Christians are not comfortable with this evil-as-mystery approach and immediately assert that while evil is a mystery to us, it is not a mystery to God. This undoubtedly is true, but it is also true that such a statement does nothing to take away the stinging fact that it *is* a mystery to *us*! A related strategy for some Christians is to explain evil by the story of the Fall in Genesis. But the Genesis story, like Jesus' parrying of the question about those who died in Siloam, simply *acknowledges* the reality of evil. The story does not *explain* it. After all, why was there a snake in the garden of Eden in the first place? The

Genesis account does not explain this. It eloquently asserts that there are elements of creation that can inhibit our flourishing as human beings. So we are stuck with a mystery, but we are still free to choose how to interpret this mystery.

The fact that we have the freedom to choose how to interpret our mysteries is part of the larger mystery itself. The Christian story, however, tells us that we are not left alone with the choice. God's grace comes to us and whispers words of direction. We can hear them if, as the Bible says, we have "ears to hear." Sooner or later, we are beckoned out of our numbness. In my work after the plane crash I was reminded that for Christians, it is gratitude and joy that often do the beckoning.

## The Mystery of Death
## Meets the Mystery of Life

In the building where the survivors were taken after the plane crash, two of the plane's flight attendants stood in the hallway. I began speaking to one named Susan who still had on her blood-spattered service apron. As we spoke, she started crying and we hugged. I led her into an office down the hall where we sat opposite each other and cried together. After we sat for a while in tears, I asked her if she would like to call someone.

At this point, the telephone lines were not yet in use (though shortly they would be tied up by the press seeking information). I got an outside line, and Susan said that she wanted to try to call her father. She asked me to dial. As she told me the numbers, I punched each one, and within one ring an anxious male voice answered the phone. Even though he just said "Hello," concern and worry were clearly evident in his voice. I said, "Is this Mr. White?" He said "Yes." I said, "There is someone here who wants to speak to you," and I handed the phone to Susan.

She took the phone, and I was standing next to her when she spoke the words, "Dad? . . . I'm alive!"

The tears came again for Susan, for me, and for her father. This time, however, somehow the tears were transmuted, transposed into a different key compared to the tears we cried together before the telephone call. Now the tears we were crying were not just the tears of emptiness, shock, grief, and disbelief. Now the tears had an element, a small but unmistakable element, of joy.

"Dad? . . . I'm alive!"

We were standing in the midst of death, but were now looking out at life. Susan did not choose to say anything other than that most basic affirmation that a living person could make—"I'm alive!"—but the words had unspeakable power. *I am alive in the midst of death. Breath has been breathed into me.*

Susan did not say "*I'm* alive!" She was not making a comparative statement; she was not making a judgment about the superiority of one person over another. Nor was it a statement of pride, of "look at me, I made it and others didn't." Susan said "I'm *alive*!" It was the simple and naked utterance that life makes—that fully awake, fully aware life must make. "I'm alive."

The element of joy in that cry from the heart was the element of joy that is inherent in life. This joy proclaims that life is a gift. She spoke the words to one who in a human sense helped give her this gift of life, her father.

In one sense the words are silly and can be easily mocked—if she were speaking on the phone, of course she would be alive. Who in their right mind would ever say such a thing? Yet, truer words, more profound words, more important words, have never been spoken. She was in her right mind, and her mind perceived, and her heart perceived, and her lips spoke of that ultimate mystery. "I'm alive."

Susan's naming of this truth, through tears of gratitude, in the midst of the broken mystery of life, was as genuine an act of worship as I have ever witnessed. Through those words she invoked the awe-filled presence of God which turned that office into a holy place. The holiness that filled the office was more intense than that invoked by the most beautiful landscape or the most majestic cathedral. It was, in fact, filled with the holiness of Eden. "I'm alive."

This joy that Susan named, the grateful joy that celebrates the sheer fact of life—the joy that leads to worship—must be put into dialogue with the numbness of Rachel and Peter. In due time, this joy must confront not only the numbness of mystery, but all of the very real anger, sorrow, grief and broken-heartedness of life. Only when this very real joy is put together with the very real sorrow can the Christian view of the mystery of life be complete.

When we do not deny either of these two sides of our mysterious reality, then we can, like Job before us, look straight into the deepest mysteries of life and confess that there are "things too wonderful for me to know" (Job 42:3, NIV). Knowing that life is *supposed* to be a mystery, and that it is *not* just our personal intellectual or spiritual shortcomings that make it seem so, can help revive us and equip us for the next installment of the mystery. When we realize that life is both a mystery and a gift, then we can once again push our boat back into the swift currents of lived experience with hope. The route may be uncharted, but with God's divine wind in our sails, we can trust enough to take the rudder that is offered.

QUESTIONS FOR REFLECTION AND MEDITATION

- If the idea of living in the midst of mysteries seems foreign to you, consider some of the central stories of the Bible. Read the stories of the first few chapters of Genesis (both the Creation and Fall), the story of Job, and the Passion accounts of Jesus. Reflect on how each of these *describes* mystery far more than they *explain* mystery. How can these stories that describe great mysteries shape our own response to mystery?

- Consider whether it is easier in your own life to live in a pretense of comfort and certainty rather than to face the reality of mystery. How can naming the truth about the reality of mystery in our lives be a comforting resource for facing tragedy? How can putting an end to denial free our energies for more creative use?

- How can you name the reality of mystery in your own life? Can you see it manifesting itself both in things that you fear and things that you love?

- If you are facing the mystery of tragedy, try to put the tragedy into your own words. What particularly is tragic? What happened that you sense should not have happened? Honestly name your responses to the tragedy.

These might include fear, grief, sorrow, anger, and other unpleasant emotions. While these reactions can be extremely troubling, they are normal responses to tragedy, even for a Christian. Try to place these emotions in a larger context of the mystery of life. Consciously choose and name the mystery that you want to define your life.

- How does the mystery of life-as-a-gift interact with the mystery of tragedy in your own life? Does one cancel out the other, or is the interplay more subtle? Can you see the possibility of holding on to *both* mysteries as a dramatic and life-giving challenge, or must one or the other finally prevail?

# TEARS

$S$hortly after the rescue coordinators took Susan and the rest of the survivors off the air base, I hitched a ride back to my home in Le Mars, arriving there about 10:00 at night. Since I had just happened to be near the airport when the plane crashed and was in civilian clothes, I donned my chaplain's uniform at home. There my wife told me that she had taken our daughters to the movie *Peter Pan* that afternoon, although her thoughts remained on the plane crash. Knowing that my family was home safe helped me to get in the car and drive back to the crash scene. I started circulating among the security police who guarded the crash site overnight.

The rescue workers felt strongly that we should have recovered the bodies immediately after removing all of the survivors. The FAA and the NTSB, though, told us that the bodies must remain where they lay until the next morning. This upset many people who felt that leaving the bodies on the ground overnight seemed somehow unholy. Yet we had to live with the decision.

As a result of the decision, the security police from my Air National Guard unit had to set up a perimeter around the area to guard against looters and curiosity seekers. No such incidents were reported, but much activity kept us busy. The busyness, though, had a lot more to do with human brokenheartedness than with criminal activity. When we keep vigil with the dead, we hear much noisy silence.

When the sun rose the next morning, many grisly and heartbreaking scenes were visible. At the sight of one of them, I broke down and cried. A man and a boy, apparently father and son, had died with the man's arms wrapped around the boy. They died in an embrace of love.

As I stood there crying, a security policeman asked if I was okay. I said "Yes" and thanked him for his concern. I continued to cry. I could think of nothing more "okay" to do.

In the early morning we began removing the bodies from the crash site. The doctors from the FAA, officials from the NTSB, the state medical examiner, and hundreds of volunteers assembled at the crash site and went about the process of photographing the bodies, putting the bodies in bags, and then taking them to the morgue. After the removal of the bodies, the volunteers spent their time recovering the United States mail that had been on board, then pieces of the fuselage, and everything else from the crash site.

Most of the volunteers came from our Air National Guard unit, but dozens of other organizations also contributed to the effort. We were an accessible source of disciplined workers willing to take direction and ready to help. As over one hundred of us united to begin this recovery, I stood up in the back of a pick-up truck on the runway, and I asked the volunteers to join in prayer. No objections came. I read the Twenty-third Psalm, for it seemed that we really were in the valley of the shadow of death. When I read the psalm and prayed, I was filled with tears and my voice cracked and broke. Part of me was embarrassed at not being more "professional." But another part of me simply said "be who you are." I was, and the tears came.

A few days after the crash I went to Saint Luke's Hospital with four members of my unit to make connections with people they had pulled out of the plane. One interaction was particularly memorable. When the father of two rescued boys found out that the two people from my unit standing before him had carried his sons out of the plane, he began weeping, saying, "You have given me back my family." The rescuers felt the gratitude that was in the heart of the father, and their presence there gave him a chance to express it in a concrete way through his tears, through his embrace.

Bringing those who cry together with those who elicit those tears made our trip to the hospital an awe-filled time. Kierkegaard once said that we owe it to those we love to express our love to them, for they are the ones who engendered love within us. So it is with gratitude. To be in the midst of such connections between grateful ones and those to whom they are grateful is to be on holy ground.

Of course, to write about such things is to run the risk of not doing them justice. This is true especially if we try to make objective what finally can be only subjective, which is one of the problems with the coverage by the news media of tragedies. Thankfully, some reporters know the limits of their objectifying medium.

During the hospital reunion, a camera crew from one of the local television stations was ready to cover the reunion until the reporter saw that the depth of what was taking place went beyond the scope of what he felt comfortable recording. He took the lens of the camera and pointed it to the ground and said to his cameraman "No, that's too personal." By and large, I found that attitude to be prevalent among the local reporters. A different attitude prevailed among the national press.

That too says something about our appropriation of real tragedy and mystery in our lives. The national press had swooped in to cover the flames and the smoke, the death and the injury, the rescue and the heroics. After a short time they were gone. The local press, of course, had to be there before, during, and after the crash; they had to live with many of those about whom they reported. Perhaps that closeness necessitates more attention to the human side of the event. There is less of the glibness, less of seeing the event in larger categories ("another airplane crash...," "another instance that raises the question of airline safety....") The local press knew that this was something that affected people, particular people with names that they knew. For them, the event had a subjective side, the side of the broken heart, a side marked by tears.

## "VULNERABLE" OR "REAL"?

Some might say that openly crying is showing one's "vulnerability," that to cry in front of others is to be "vulnerable." That word *vulnerable* has a lot of currency in conversations about pastoring and counseling, and I have used it from time to time. I do not think, though, that the term "vulnerable" is as good or accurate as the word "real." When we are real, we may or may not be vulnerable. Vulnerability has to do with a perception of danger in the environment that could cause you harm. To be "vulnerable" is to say that you are concerned with potential "attacks" by others.

To be "real," on the other hand, is to be concerned with being true to *your* experience. Whether or not that makes you "vulnerable" depends on the character of those who surround you. Your being real may elicit attacks, mockery, and sarcasm, or it may elicit empathy, care, and compassion. The reaction of those who encounter your reality is finally a function of the kind of people that those people choose to be, not a function of who you are. Being real can make one vulnerable, but it should be our desire for living truthfully that compels us to be real, not a concern to either seek or avoid vulnerability.

## Heart Religion

The day after the crash, Colonel Dennis Swanstrom, my base commander, asked me to coordinate a joint worship service with the Sioux City Fire Department chaplain. It was to be for all the workers involved with the crash and rescue effort. I decided it would be best to have the worship service after we had removed the bodies from the field. By doing this there would be some sense of completion of at least one of the important tasks before us, even though the morgue would be in place for many more days. The Fire Department Chaplain, Father Brown; a retired Air Guard Chaplain, Father Boes; and I led the service. We sang a couple of simple hymns. We read scripture and presented a brief homily. I spoke on three of the beatitudes—blessed are those who are poor in spirit, blessed are those who mourn, and blessed are those who show mercy.

The following Sunday I led worship on the grass outside the dining hall. My sermon was on tragedy and our response to it. The passage I focused on was from Romans 12:15: "Rejoice with those who rejoice, weep with those who weep."

The power of this simple Bible verse had been lost on me until after the plane crash. The strength of it was first pointed out to me by another Air Guard Chaplain, Bob Hicks, in the context of a conference of chaplains. He was talking about his ministry in the aftermath of a Delta Airlines crash in Dallas a few years earlier. How assaulting on our pride as theologians, ministers, Christians, to think that what we are called to do with victims is to weep with them. "Weep with those who weep."

"Certainly," we might think, "we should be able to offer a profound word, put the tragedy in the big picture, explain things in a way so that we can make it all better." The Apostle Paul simply invites us to weep. Many will quickly mock this as a silly, sentimental response. But we need to see that weeping is merely a sentimental response only if it is our *sole* response. The genuine, heartfelt compassion that can lead to tears is a necessary root of any other response that might follow.

Here is a clear example of what I understand to be true heart religion. Heart religion is not content to remain within the heart. Heart religion acts as a disposition for other behaviors: it is a motivation for action. But the heart, the center of who we are—that which shows what we love and hate and fear and take joy in—this center must be engaged in order for us to be true Christians. Weeping is an unmistakable sign that we are engaged.

When we weep, we tell the world what we value. When we weep with others who weep, we tell them, by our tears, that we see things the way that they see them. We tell them that we see reality, and we see the mystery, and we see the tragedy, and it breaks our hearts too. Before they started pestering Job with their finger-pointing theologies, his friends "sat with him on the ground seven days and seven nights, and no one spoke a word to him, for they saw that his suffering was very great" (Job 2:13). These friends would have done better if they had never opened their mouths and simply wept with Job.

On Wednesday, August 9, almost three weeks after the crash, we held a worship service at Morningside College auditorium. This was intended as a community worship service, and so the planners felt that it was appropriate to broadcast it locally. Instead of one sermon, six short stories were told at this service. The stories illustrated the various kinds of involvement in the tragedy by different segments of the community. Two hospitals, the fire department, the two colleges that offered housing to the victims' relatives, and the Air National Guard were represented. At the request of the base commander, I represented the Air National Guard.

The story I told reflected what I had encountered when the sun came up the morning after the crash, the scene that moved me to tears and caused the security policeman to ask if I were okay. The memory I recalled at that worship service remains vivid in my mind to this day: the image of the man embracing the young boy—his arms encircling the young boy from behind in a gesture of love. That those two should die in such a graphic embrace of love was heart-breaking to behold. The image had a power and integrity of its own, but it also symbolized something else. It symbolized Jesus Christ dying on the cross for us.

In our Christian faith, we understand the death of Jesus to show that God has taken on all of the features of our existence on earth, including death. That God would become enfleshed, incarnate, would become a human being and die with us identifies our Lord with an unspeakably powerful way. God's loving presence enfolded Jesus in his birth, his ministry of teaching and healing, and especially his death on the cross. Because of this, Jesus enfolds us with his cross-stretched arms and nail-pierced hands in both our living and our dying, just as the man encircled the young boy at the time of death with his arms of love.

Why should we weep with those who weep? Because Jesus showed God's love for us by weeping with us in our weeping and dying with us in our dying. Such weeping is not a mistake, or a reason for embarrassment—it is instead one of the most important spiritual resources available to us. We are not in control in such traumatic circumstances. I think we often go to great extents in our minds and our emotions to try to rationalize our lack of control. We are not in control of the reality of which we are a small part, and our powerlessness leads us to tears.

In crying, we acknowledge our lack of control, our inability to have things the way we want them. In crying, we are not failing to be strong; we are being strong enough to acknowledge our weakness, our humanness. A friend once said that tears in such a situation are really a form of prayer to God, a confession of our limitedness, our humanity. I think that statement contains great truth. In such situations, tears are the bodily expression of humility. Tears are our humble acknowledgment that while we are beings created by God in God's image, we are not God. When we cry those kind of tears we are being real, and being real is a necessary step toward the threshold of real holiness. That threshold is humility.

## QUESTIONS FOR REFLECTION AND MEDITATION

- Do you see crying as a mistake, a breakdown of meaning, a disruption of normalcy, or do you see it as a natural and expected part of life?

- What do you make of the scriptures where God is depicted in anguish over the sufferings of God's people? Is such passion in God an embarrassing part of the scriptures, or should it instead judge our own projections about a stoic, unmoved God?

- What is the meaning for our lives of the fact that Jesus Christ, God incarnate, wept on certain occasions? How should we interpret the everyday ups and downs of our inner lives if we confess that Jesus became a human being just like us in every way except that he was without sin? Do you, unconsciously perhaps, think that the emotional life, filled as it is with crying and laughing, is dumb or even sinful? Why?

- Reflect on the difference between a sympathy that ends up weakening the victim and a compassion that ennobles and builds up the victim. How can you describe in real life what words and actions surround each of these so that we might avoid the one and foster the other?

- A philosopher once described laughing and crying as "boundary experiences" of our lives. How can we understand our tears in the face of mystery as an example of this?

- In your own encounter with tragedy, reflect on your own periods of numbness, intense crying, or even hysterical laughter as boundary experiences of your life. What were you on the boundary of?

# HUMILITY

During one brief devotion that I gave for the rescue workers after the plane crash, I read from Luke 10, the Good Samaritan story. I told all the workers assembled there that they were in fact good Samaritans; they were helping the unknown travelers, just as the man in the parable had. They were performing helpful and needed tasks.

But I also told them while they are good Samaritans, they are not angels. They are flesh and blood with real hurts because of what they had just gone through and what they continued to experience. I emphasized to them that they should not deny the feelings that have arisen because of their experiences and that they need to share these feelings with somebody else—counselors, chaplains, others who went through the experience. I especially encouraged them to share their feelings with God, to speak the truth that was in their hearts, for it is when we open our hearts to God that the healing can begin.

One of the most striking features of the many heart-opening counseling sessions that followed—and one of the greatest surprises in my whole ministry—was the widespread sense of guilt among the rescue workers.

We do not know much—nothing, in fact—about what may or may not have gone on inside of the good Samaritan. Jesus' parable was not concerned with giving us insight into such things. The parable is to show who was the true neighbor, who treated the robbed and beaten man as if he were valuable and loved. Jesus says it was the Samaritan, a member of a people hated by the Jews. The one who was the outsider was the most helpful.

As the traveler was helped on the road between Jerusalem and Jericho, so were these people on Flight 232 from Denver to Chicago helped between their origin and their destination. The people of Sioux City and the surrounding areas, strangers to all on board, stopped and took the initiative to help these travelers. Surely the people who helped were neighbors—if not in the geographical sense—certainly in the sense that Jesus called his followers to be.

But what of the inner life of those who helped in Sioux City? The biblical parable points us merely to who was of help and tells us nothing of the effects of helping. I was to find out.

## Encountering God through Our Limitations

"If I had only done something more, maybe more people would have survived." "I just have a sense that I could have done something else, something more than what I did." Such statements came from even the most involved, the most heroically committed people, those whose behavior was the marvel of many.

In such counseling situations, I believe the first and most appropriate response to such statements is to hear them out, to let the people open themselves up and show who they were and what they were experiencing. In the process of this listening, I tried to give support and reassurance that every person did the best that he or she could do in such an incredibly stressful situation. The truth is that I do honestly believe that all *did* do the absolute best of which they were capable, which sometimes entailed making the mature judgment that they had taken all they could take and it was time to leave.

There were those members of my unit who did not go out to the crash site, who did not help collect the bodies, who did not help in the morgue. There were those in our unit who said "no" to the request for help. For some of those people their decision has been a very hard thing to deal with. But it is my deepest conviction that everyone on that first day, and during the following weeks, did all that they could do. It is my conviction that everyone did what he or she should have done.

Those who knew they were not prepared to enter into such a scene—those who knew that such trauma was not for them—were exercising mature judgment and doing the best thing they could do. It would have done no one any good for those people to push themselves beyond their own limits and to end up simply adding to the chaos.

While my role as a counselor and minister defined my action as primarily listening and hearing these people voice their guilt, my vocation as a theologian spurred me to reflect on the phenomenon of guilt. I needed to understand not just the guilt of those who did not answer the call but more especially the guilt of those who did.

"Survivor guilt" is a fairly well-known phenomenon. One thinks of the numerous stories of people who have survived death camps during World War II, or people who have survived tragedies like this plane crash, people who were on board, later asking "Why me? Why was I saved while my friends, family, loved ones were killed?" Survivor guilt was understandable to me, but "hero guilt" was a new one for me.

Normally, in our everyday lives, we do not want to think about traumatic situations. When we do, is it not commonly our tendency to fantasize and think that if something traumatic did happen to us we could somehow "make it all right?" I know it is true for me and, from my work after the plane crash, it seems that it is not an uncommon feeling.

But then, when we actually are in such a traumatic situation, we find that we are *not* God. We are limited mortals who cannot fix everything and make it all better, no matter how hard we try.

Is this guilt that arises from such situations not ultimately related to our anxiety over our own limitedness, our finitude? Does such guilt not reflect the denial of the realities of human life and, finally, the denial of death?

## TALKING ABOUT IT

Some people after the crash took the attitude of "Why talk about what we went through; there are no answers to the 'big' questions, so why not try to just put it behind us?" The truth seems to be that people do, in general, want to talk about it—but only when they are ready to do so. Why is it so important to talk? Secular counseling will speak of "venting" the emotions as if they were primarily a kind of pressurized hot air that needs to escape. What I see in this process of talking about our experiences, though, is more than what this "escape valve" image presents. In talking about our experiences there can be an implicit appropriation of the deepest theological understanding of what it means to be a frail, fragile, and mortal human being.

Why is this apparently innocuous—some even think "gossipy"—process of "talking about it" important theologically? From a Christian standpoint we talk about these experiences—push them into the verbal realm—because Christianity is not a religion of intuition. The academic way of putting this is that there is a "positivity" to Christianity.

Contrary to what some of the classic liberal theologians (such as Friedrich Schleiermacher) and Transcendentalists thought, Christianity comes as a *revelation* to natural human beings. It is not something that we could guess or design on our own by rooting around in our interior life. The idea that God came into the world in the person of Jesus Christ, died on the cross for the forgiveness of our sins, was raised from the dead, and then sent the Holy Spirit to affect our daily lives, is not something that one develops on one's own. The truth of Christianity—and more to the point, the truth about *being a Christian*—does not come as a result of intuiting universal truths or cleverly speculating about what one might expect. Becoming a Christian means learning a set of specific and contingent behaviors—intellectual, physical, and, yes, even emotional behaviors. Becoming a Christian means learning an entire way of life.

Talking about our experiences can, ideally at least, be more than just "venting." *Christian* counseling, whether by professionals or by loving Christian friends, does not involve just "letting off steam." It is a processing, a shaping of our experience, and putting our experience into understandable categories that come from the Christian tradition.

This "processing" is something less exalted (but perhaps ultimately more important) than "explaining." When we talk about our traumas and tragedies—and the real limitations of our response to them—we are studying in the school of humility. As Merlin told King Arthur in *Camelot*, the best thing for being sad is to learn something. If we can learn something from our trauma about who we are and how God chooses to be in this world, our sadness will not disappear, but it will at least be *used* and not merely left to fester like an unlanced boil. When this is done, we are not only processing our experiences, we are redeeming them.

But that is *not* to say that we go through pain to "learn a lesson from God." There is a lot more pain in the world than there are lessons to be learned about this world. We must finally identify with Job and not his "comforters" on such issues. No answers will satisfy that largest question of "why?" There is no "explaining" in that sense. However, contrary to the fears born of our pretensions, humbly admitting our ignorance, humbly admitting that evil is finally something that does not submit to our explanations—admitting that tragedy and evil are mysteries—is in fact the best solace we can offer, to ourselves or others. It is the only thing that rings true.

A psychologist once told a story about a patient who feared stepping outside his house. This fear so ruled his life that he found himself driven to the brink of suicide. Finally, when he could take no more, he decided he would kill himself by stepping out of the house, certain that the explosion of anxiety within him caused by this act would kill him. He opened the door and stepped out. The anxiety was almost unbearable, and yet he continued out of the house, up the street, out to an open field. To his surprise, he did not die, and, in fact, was cured of this anxiety.

Confronting our fears, naming who we are in our humble and limited existences, does not increase the anxiety and fear; it frees us from them as it did for this patient. Our concealed weakness, and our self-hatred for having that weakness, can keep us from allowing God into our lives. Our prideful refusal to acknowledge who we really are closes the door to God.

Acknowledging our limits in the face of mystery has nothing to do with sin, though we all too often link sin and our limitations. In talking about our spiritual lives in a Christian context, we must be clear about what sin is and what it is not. Sin is the affront to God that humans engage in when they act as if God is not real. The greatest species of sin, as understood in the Christian tradition, is pride, which is the tendency to think that we ourselves are God.

When we are traumatized and shocked into realizing our limitedness, we sometimes mistake this limitedness for sinfulness, but in reality it is just the opposite. Our limitedness can be a door to the grace of God. When we give up our pretensions of being in charge of all of reality, and even our own lives (at least many important aspects of our own lives), we can begin to worship the One who created us. We also stop worshiping the insecure projections of our narcissism. The particular temptations to pride and thinking that we are God will come in a variety of forms depending on our own history and our own pattern of brokenness. It is not the *fact* of our limitedness and our brokenness that is sinful, but it is our sad, insecure attempt to *hide* our limitedness and brokenness which manifests our sinfulness.

It is not sinful to have a particular pattern of brokenness, a particular history. Such brokenness is the essence of being real, historical, temporal beings. Our histories only become sinful to us when we, out of our own overweening pride, try to deny their reality. I can name this dynamic because I have seen it operating in my own life.

One of the assumptions I have lived with was that I was not to value my feelings. Is that a "male thing," or is it more generally a middle class American's understanding of life? Is it, perhaps, a function of my own family life as a child? I do not know. But there is a wider intellectual and cultural atmosphere, a leftover from the Enlightenment, which tells us that the individual's experience is to be ignored in favor of the "objectively" true REALITY. (People who talk this way do tend to speak in capital letters.) For whatever reason, downplaying the particular features of my own individual history was a very real tendency for me.

Part of this avoidance of strong feelings seemed to be tied up with the assumption that if I allowed a conscious awareness of something bad, such as despair, then there would be no returning from it. Riding one mood until it dropped, like a cowboy riding a horse to exhaustion, seemed to be the way I proceeded, and there was the fear that a bad mood—once acknowledged—would never drop, would never become exhausted.

I finally realized, though, that what really held me was fear. The fear that a deeply felt emotion would never leave kept me from allowing conscious awareness of my feelings. In this state, I felt only fear to the exclusion of all other emotions. Through helping others process and shape their own experience after the plane crash, though, I was able to let go of some of my own fear and more gracefully to enter into my own history, my own heart.

When I reflect on my own heart's story and my own attempts to be a good Samaritan, I have to say that I received many rewards and blessings throughout this time of ministry. I am not talking about the public and private words of thanks, or even the medals I received from the state of Iowa and the federal government. When people open themselves up to you and share their deepest fears, sorrows and hopes—in short, when they share their hearts with you—you have been granted a sacred trust, almost a kind of sacrament. Especially moving to me was when people shared their memories of past tragedies that had been triggered by the present tragedy.

Repeatedly during counseling about the trauma of the present, images of past traumas were conjured up in the memories of those I counseled. These images included wars, previous fires, car crashes, and even deaths in the family. It seems that in some sense all trauma is cumulative, and we carry our past traumas with us in one form or another. When the men and women I counseled opened themselves up to me in such ways, sharing what is most intimate in their lives by sharing their past traumas, it was an invitation into sacred space where God pours out transforming and renewing grace. When people are most real—when they are defenseless, when they can offer no conditions for love—that is when our most unconditional love is elicited, and to have that love elicited from us is to be blessed.

## MINISTRY IN HUMILITY

But it was not only in the midst of the intensities of counseling or even in our gathered worship that I felt blessed to be serving God. I am sure that it was service in God's name to take young Peter to the bathroom in the hours after the crash. Everyone, and there were literally hundreds who did those kinds of small but important acts, was every bit a minister of God and of God's love as I was when I was performing my various "professional" activities.

Let me take that line of thought a step further. Though it assaults my pride in my cognitive abilities and theological learning to admit this, I think I was probably never more clearly a minister than when I broke down in front of the security policeman and wept at the sight of the man and boy, embracing as they died. Or when I read a Psalm with a quaking voice to all of the workers on the runway in the midst of all the bodies.

There are many different ways of being a minister. Sometimes, maybe always, what is needed most is some-body simply to be a human being, the human that Christ calls us to be. If we have been formed in the Christian way of life, we can really be "there"—focused, centered, and present in the pain. If we can do that, we have ministered. Sometimes the best we can "do" is to "be." Perhaps at times the simplest gesture of caring best conveys the church's message.

In our confessions as Christians, we need to name more than the sinfulness that calls for God's forgiveness and our brokenness which calls for healing. What is most important for good Samaritans (whether they are professionals such as firefighters and chaplains, or laypeople simply acting out the Christian vocation of friendship) is that we name and confess our limitedness, our humanity. We confess that we are not God and we know it. Our limitedness, our *humanness,* should not be occasion for guilt. Our awareness is an opening through which we can receive the grace of God.

To be broken-hearted, to embody true humility, is the paradoxical and radically surprising way into Christian heart religion.[1] I think this is the meaning of the word the Lord gave to Paul in 2 Corinthians 12:9: "My grace is sufficient for you, for power is made perfect in weakness." This truth is also shown in Psalm 51:17, a psalm ascribed to King David after Nathan's confrontation of the king's adultery:

*The sacrifice acceptable to God is a broken spirit; a broken and contrite heart, O God, you will not despise.*

When we make this "sacrifice" and name that we are not God, we can start trusting that the real God is already starting the process of healing, restoring, and re-creating.

---

[1] See my book *As If the Heart Mattered: A Wesleyan Spirituality* (Nashville, Tenn: Upper Room Books, 1997) where I discuss repentance and humility as the "porch" of religion.

## QUESTIONS FOR REFLECTION AND MEDITATION

- It has been said that true humility is being able to say "There is a God . . . and it is not me." How can you claim this kind of humility for yourself? When is such humility a challenge? How might your life be different if this simple sentence set your spiritual agenda every day?

- What will you have to let go of in order to deepen your humility? Are there attitudes, goals, or desires you have which are not consistent with the acknowledgment that you are a creature and not the creator?

- Some people because of the details of their personal history, tend to deny their own mortality, limitations and shortcomings. Some, on the other hand, because of their history, seem to think of *nothing but* their shortcomings and limitations. Either extreme is destructive to Christian growth. Are you closer to one extreme than the other in your usual attitude? Without denying where you are now, how can you move to a healthy humility which claims both your limitations and the hope that comes from God's power for transformation? Think of small, specific steps you can take.

• Sin needs forgiveness. Brokenness needs healing. Our limited nature calls for humility. How do these statements reflect your understanding of the human condition and God's grace? Reflect on the distinctions, and the interrelations of these three realities.

• How can your own encounter with tragedy lead you into a deeper sense of humility and the peace that comes with it?

# GENTLENESS

As I was running toward the crash site that afternoon in July, I felt all of the cleverness, all of the distanced speculation, all of the glib slickness of academia slipping off me like a large coat that no longer fit. As I ran, I did something I was not in the habit of doing—I prayed out loud with my hands in the air. As I ran, I lifted my hands to the sky and said aloud simply, "Lord, please make me an instrument of your will. Lord, please make me an instrument of your peace."

My academic research for my M.A. in philosophy and my Ph.D. in theology dealt with the nature of religious experience. In that work I explored many views and conceptions that have been formulated throughout the history of reflection on these topics. One aspect of my academic work that had a lasting influence on me was that, in the Christian tradition, intense sensations and deeply felt feelings were not finally to be highly valued unless they led to a new quality of life in the believer. The deepest kinds of life-changing encounters in spiritual reality always flowed into an extraordinary new form of everyday living. High mountaintop experiences were not necessarily good in and of themselves; they were generally not regarded as their own end by the mainstream of the tradition.

Because of this, the feeling or experiential dimension of religious life was something that engendered hesitancy, if not skepticism in my life. The world was too full of wildly deluded people who seemed to go off the deep end of experience. Though I had read many books about such experience, my own felt sensations were closely guarded.

I suppose it is because of that background that I hesitate to place too much emphasis on the feeling I experienced running into the crash scene. But, to be perfectly honest, when I prayed that prayer with my hands open, there was a kind of lightness, an emptying of fear into a friendly unknown that is hard to describe. It was an emptying, but also an empowering. I knew that I was running into something desperately tragic, and, in terms of my inventory of human resources, I was running in empty-handed. Yet I also knew that God was somehow filling my hands and my heart.

I arrived at the airport approximately fifteen minutes after the crash had occurred. At the temporary command post, I met Al Sundberg, the director of ambulances. I introduced myself as a chaplain with the Air National

Guard (I was, of course, in civilian clothes) and he said, "I'm glad you're here; I just got goose bumps shaking your hand."

Was it simply the fact that I was a clergyperson that gave him goose bumps? The idea of bringing this terrible tragedy together in his mind with the idea of God, is that what gave him goose bumps? Or could he have somehow experienced something akin to what I had experienced running in? If God had anointed me in some way, if my prayer request had somehow been met, would it be obvious to others? I did not have time to ponder those questions then.

I rode out to the crash site in an ambulance. Hopping out, I noticed bodies everywhere. One man remained strapped in his seat even though the force of the impact had torn the seat out of the fuselage. He had apparently rolled and tumbled down the runway in his seat and had come to rest on the back of his neck. He was obviously dead. I ran to the nearest group of survivors who had been laid in rows next to one another by those fire fighters and emergency medical technicians who had been first on the scene. I asked one man who was conscious what his name was, and he said, "Brad." His face was very bloody and his arms were badly gouged. I recall saying to him that he should just "breathe in God's spirit, just slowly breathe in and out. That's your job." I laid my hand on his chest gently, and we spoke briefly before I left.

Soon someone asked me to check for a pulse on a woman lying nearby. The person asking said his own pulse was racing too quickly to feel someone else's pulse. I felt the woman's clammy neck but could feel nothing. I asked if there were any survivors still trapped in the plane, and he pointed me in the direction of the cockpit.

When the plane crashed, it had tumbled down the runway, almost cartwheeling. When it finally came to rest, it was in three main sections. The main body of the fuselage had the worst fire. The tail section and the cockpit were thrown hundreds of feet from each other. By the time I arrived, the rescuers had removed the survivors from the tail section and fuselage, but the cockpit had just been discovered. It continues to be hard to imagine that the heap of wreckage that I saw then has been a cockpit. It seemed only a small hill of wires, cables, seats, sheet metal, and other debris. Around this pile of mangled and compressed wreckage, probably about twenty people were working to free the flight crew.

After I got there, the rescuers brought in a forklift to try to lift the wreckage off the backs of the crew members. While they were preparing to lift the wreckage, I spoke with one of the survivors who remained trapped. He told me his name, and I told him that I was the chaplain. He said in rather a chipper voice, "Great, thanks; I'm glad you're here." I laid my hand on his head and told him to keep breathing in God's spirit. "Keep breathing in and out. That's your job. Everybody's working as hard as they can to get you out of there." The forklift raised the wreckage, and the EMTs transported him along with the other crew members to the waiting ambulance.

In retrospect, one aspect of these first few minutes on the crash site seemed especially surprising to me. As a boy, I had heard stories of people being able to do super-human things in a moment of tragedy—people who, when confronted with terribly misshapen features of our twisted reality, were somehow able to set them right.

I remember hearing about a mother whose child was under a car when the jack holding up the car collapsed. I remember hearing with bone-chilling and heart-filling awe how the mother was somehow empowered to lift the car off the child so that the child could crawl out from underneath it. The mother's back was broken in the process, but the child lived. Surely a force beyond what was "natural" was alive in that woman. Like most who hear such stories, I longed to have that power in my life.

Yet, when I ran onto the runway on that hot, July afternoon, when I lifted my hands in the air and prayed for God to use me, there were no cars to pull off people. Sure, I helped in a small way with the physical extraction of the flight crew, briefly holding one piece of twisted metal away from a fire fighter so that he could remove the wreckage off the pilots' backs. But that was no great physical effort, nothing supernatural in that.

Instead, my experience was that when I raised my hands into the air and asked for empowerment, I was empowered . . . to be gentle.

## POWER AND GENTLENESS

Gentleness was a type of empowerment that was foreign to my natural mind. John Wayne charging up the hill, guns blazing; Rocky going back for the fifteenth round, broken and bruised yet answering the bell; the Japanese gymnast going for his full-impact dismount from the rings even though his leg is broken, because he wants his team to win; the mother lifting the car off the child—these were the striking images of empowerment that filled my mind before that day. These pictures of courage and action fed my attraction to the warrior image that goes with the military uniform. But what was my experience?

I was empowered for gentleness.

To touch the injured, the dead, the trapped, and to speak a gentle word. This was a different model of empowerment than that which the images buried in my mind had imprinted on me. The contrast between these two differing images of empowerment was striking for me. Yet, on reflection, I started to remember that I had encountered this conflict between competing understandings of empowerment before, in my own family history.

## GENTLENESS REMEMBERED

Growing up in Park Ridge, Illinois, I had a fairly conventional religious upbringing. My mother was raised a Northern Baptist and my father came out of the Church of the Brethren, but neither made much of this religious background. My mother, though, felt it was important for my brother and me to be raised in the church, so until the time we were confirmed, we were often at Sunday school and worship at the First Methodist Church of Park Ridge.

I remember being baptized when I was about seven years old, although this was not a giant, spiritual experience for me. As a matter of fact, the only thing I remember about it is that we were all lined up along the front of the church and the minister came down the row of young children, stopped by each child, and placed a small amount of water on each head, baptizing us. When he got to a girl next to me, she looked up at him and yelled out, "Don't you touch me!" The congregation broke out in laughter. That was the highlight of my baptism.

My mother taught Sunday school occasionally, but after my brother and I were confirmed, church seemed to be less of a priority for all of us. I later found out that my mother had become disillusioned with the church as a teenager when she saw some elders of her Baptist church secretly sipping moonshine at a local drugstore. Hypocrisy was the issue for her, not the alcohol. Her view of the church, expressed to us once we were confirmed, was that one does not need to go to church or to be a part of a church community to be a "good person." Perhaps it was even easier to be a good person if one did not have to be a part of such a messy, contradictory, and hypocritical group.

My father rarely attended church. I have only two memories of my father's own experience of church. One is that he once sarcastically sang a refrain from a hymn of his childhood that went something like "believing will make it so." He sang it in such a way that it was clear that he felt that such an approach to life was problematic at best and delusional and simple-minded at worst. He had become, after all, a tough-minded businessman and a successful entrepreneur in the world of commerce. In such a world, "believing" did not "make it so," but calculated shrewdness and a lot of hard work "made it so."

The other memory I have of my father's church experience is when he spoke about the footwashing ceremonies of the Church of the Brethren, the church of his youth. This was the most distinctive part of his denomination to hear him tell it, and he seemed to be vaguely embarrassed by this.

When my father was fifty-four years old, he had a major heart attack. He was a hard-driving business man who, as president of a recording studio, had plenty of reasons to implode. The call of commerce had been strong in his life. He sometimes told my brother and me about how, as a boy, he delivered ice and newspapers to help make ends meet during the depression. He and his friend, Bill Putnam, had started the recording studio after World War II. They soon began to get some important work with Patti Page and Duke Ellington, going on to record a few "Top 40" hits like Gene Chandler's "Duke of Earl" and the Shadows of Knight's "Gloria," but making most of their money recording the sound tracks for television and radio commercials.

With the coming of financial success came the usual temptations of the world. My parents' marriage had not been a strong one at the time of my dad's heart attack. The glitz and glamour of downtown Chicago made the homelife of suburban Park Ridge seem pale in my Dad's eyes. The heart attack brought quite a change.

As my mother recounts it, there was a marked difference in his attitude toward her in those few short months between his first heart attack in May and his death in November. The man who was a shrewd promoter in the cutthroat world of the entertainment and advertising industries, the feared contract negotiator, the man who rubbed elbows with the rich and famous, was confined to his bed in the suburbs. He was dependent on his once-scorned wife, and he underwent a transformation.

Being on the receiving end of care and concern recalled to my father's mind memories of his childhood. While much of his family life growing up was painful, he had vivid memories of his Grandma Clapper. She was, he said, one who was always busy doing kindnesses for others. She would visit the sick and take care of them, take food to the hungry, and generally give her time, her energy, her presence, to those who needed it. She belonged to the Church of the Brethren, the ones who washed feet.

At the end of his life, my dad was no longer embarrassed by the feet-washers of this world. He said that my mom was one of them, and there was a reconnection in their marriage before he died. His death occurred six months after his first heart attack, but not before he had experienced the power of gentleness in a way that reunited him with the best of his past, and brought a kind of wholeness to his life.

Remembering the conflict between the power of the world that my dad pursued and the power of gentleness that my mom showed him helped me to understand my own experience with the plane crash, and I was able to name something that had only been tacit up to that point.

Truly gentle people, which does not mean weak people, but people real enough to be absolutely gentle, have always brought me to tears. Like my father before me, I was not able to name the power of that gentleness until God called me to be a part of it first hand. This gentleness is not the power of people who feign powerlessness. It is neither the power of the passive-aggressive or that of the manipulator, but the gentleness that comes from the power of God.

We say that the Holy Spirit is the spirit that Jesus somehow brought into the world in a special way. But what *was* the spirit of Jesus? It can be seen when Jesus faced down the crowd ready to stone the woman taken in adultery, and when he sent the woman on her way, forgiven and free. It is the Spirit that Jesus embodied when he who could have brought forth legions of angels to prevent his crucifixion, instead went to the cross, and on the cross asked for forgiveness for his tormentors.

This Spirit is not of this world but it comes from God. The Spirit of gentleness comes into the world in ways that we often do not expect. It comes as a helpless baby in a hick town in Palestine. It comes as a grandmother who washes feet. It comes as a wife who cares for a wayward husband. It comes in a call to a ministry of gentleness on a runway full of death.

Here, then, was the drama and challenge that attracted me to the warrior image, but the "weapon" I was called to use was not one I would have predicted. The "weapon" of gentleness showed me how the life of the Spirit can be as surprising and demanding as a charge into enemy territory with guns blazing. The amazing power of God's agenda of gentleness and presence makes all other calls to arms pale in comparison.

A part of me says that it is too self-serving to name that power in my own life, to say that the work that I did participated in the reality of God's gentleness. But, in the end, it is false modesty to deny it, for such gentleness truly comes as a gift. Having received such a gift, we cannot boast! No, when speaking of a gift, it is the giver who is to be praised. (See 1 Corinthians 4:7.)

To this God, who sends gentleness into the midst of our tragically broken lives, to *this* God be the glory, for from this God is surely the real power of our lives.

QUESTIONS FOR REFLECTION AND MEDITATION

- Have you seen gentleness as weakness or a character strength? How do you understand Galatians 5:22-24 where gentleness is considered to be a "fruit of the Spirit."

- Can you name in your own experience the witness of a truly gentle person? If so, how did his or her witness affect you? Can you name specific instances of gentleness that you would want to emulate?

- Try to describe in some detail one who acts weak in order to manipulate someone's sympathies as opposed to someone who is truly gentle.

- In what ways is God gentle? Consider the way that Jesus comported himself in the world. Can we model our life in this way? If not, what obstacles are in our way?

- How can gentleness find a place in your own response to tragedy? How are gentleness, humility, and the tears of compassion linked in a Christian response to tragedy?

# HOPE

A committee of community leaders coordinated the one-year anniversary events surrounding the crash of United Airlines Flight 232. The people on the committee thought it would be appropriate to have a memorial service one year, to the day and even the hour, after the crash. The committee asked me to lead the worship service and I accepted.

Hundreds of people gathered that rainy afternoon to take part in this worship service. As jets from our Air National Guard unit flew overhead in a "missing man" formation, there was a time for silent reflection, a time for mourning, a time for opening the heart to God. The people came for a variety of reasons. Some came to see where their relatives had died. Some came to thank those who helped pull them from the plane. Some were workers who had pulled the dead and dying and survivors from the plane. Some came to cry. Some came not knowing why.

But for many, there was a deep undercurrent of thanksgiving, and that is why the words of thanks that were given by many during the worship service—including the captain of the crashed plane, Al Haynes—had a very powerful impact.

Those who gathered there were invited to open their hearts, to name the grief and sorrow, perhaps even the anger, and then to put it all into a context of thanksgiving. Yes, "thank you" to the workers for doing their jobs. "Thanks" to the fire fighters and police, nurses and doctors, the everyday office workers, all who lent a hand that day one year ago. But this was a *worship* service. This meant that the thanksgiving was not just directed to the people, but ultimately to God. This thanksgiving and gratitude lead us to the edge of that which we cannot name when we are caught in the depths of tragedy. This gratitude leads us to the edge of hope.

## GRATITUDE FOR THE GIFT OF LIFE

How can we understand such a thing—to give thanks to God in the midst of memories of such loss and grief, suffering and death? This service was nothing less than a communal chance to express the thanksgiving that was manifested by Susan White, the flight attendant, when she spoke to her dad on the telephone the day of the crash. The thanksgiving that was part of that worship service is directly linked to those basic words, naked in their primitive joy: "I'm alive," those words which seem to say "Thank you, God, for this beautiful and deeply mysterious gift."

I did not know if Susan White would attend the memorial service in Sioux City. I knew that many of the crew members were returning as well as many passengers. But I did not know Susan would be there, and I did not really have any reason to expect that she would remember me. For who was I but a person who talked to her briefly and helped her make a phone call? It was, of course, an encounter that I would never forget, but after everything she had gone through, I did not have any reason to believe that she would remember me.

It was with great joy then that, in a receiving line held at Briar Cliff College for those crew and passengers who were returning for the service, I saw Susan again. I recognized her right away, and my heart was filled when she recognized me and said, "Oh, Chaplain Clapper" and gave me a big hug. She had brought her fiance, Dan Callender, with her, and the three of us talked briefly and joyfully there at the reception.

After the memorial service concluded, I again saw Susan and Dan, and at that time they asked me something that made me a little light-headed and my knees a little shaky. When we were talking at the base headquarters,

Susan and Dan told me that they were to be married the following summer. They then asked if I would officiate at their wedding.

Susan had remembered who I was, and she wanted me to be a part of one of the most joyous events in her life. That offer touched me deeply. It was so powerful that I could not believe it at first.

At the time when they asked me to marry them, I thought that it might have been a passing kind word to share with me. Perhaps this request was an attempt to be polite, I thought. Shortly thereafter, however, I received several phone calls and letters that showed their strong desire for me to perform the ceremony. They flew to Sioux City where we did some pre-marital counseling and planning. They met Jody and our daughters, Laura and Jenna, and we shared a very happy meal together.

That following June they sent tickets for Jody and me to fly to Wadsworth, Ohio. I co-officiated at their wedding along with Susan's hometown Lutheran pastor. During the ceremony itself, I talked about how I met Susan at the crash and how she asked me to be a part of her wedding. I did not say a lot about the whole crash experience, but my participation was in itself a testimony to the impact that crash had on Susan's life.

Susan's inclusion of me in her wedding said to all the world that the crash of United 232 was a life-changing event for her. Not only did it change her life, but Susan wanted to lift up that event and the changes that flowed from it. She wanted to name it in a very real, embodied way in the presence of God and her friends, her family, and her soon-to-be family. The life that she claimed when she said "I'm alive" was now a life that she was sharing in a new way with Dan. The quality and texture of her life would now forever be changed for having come through the crash. Her gratitude for the gift of life was now one of the master passions of her life. Because of the transition that the crash had begun, it made sense for the crash to be represented at her wedding by my presence.

Two months before Susan and Dan's wedding, I was involved in another crash-related wedding. This wedding was also personally humbling, powerful, and awe-filled. This was the wedding of Teresa Kilburn.

## NEW LIFE

Teresa Kilburn worked full-time for the Air National Guard in the area of supply. She mainly worked behind a computer and figured out how to make that machine and its complicated software perform. When the plane crashed, Teresa was in a marriage that was very unhealthy, and she had fallen into the labyrinth of alcohol abuse. Teresa had started to climb out of this downward spiral when Flight 232 crashed in Sioux City.

With such a large plane coming in with so many passengers on board, the rescuers knew they could use all the help available. The "all-call" went out over the base loudspeaker for anyone who could possibly help to come to the runway. Teresa, the office worker and computer operator, responded to the call. Teresa—with the bad marriage, Teresa the alcoholic, Teresa with low self esteem—answered the call.

In the hours and days after she answered the call, Teresa saw and experienced things that she had never even imagined. Seeing the injured and dying, seeing the dead on the field and in the morgue, Teresa could have folded up. Someone untrained in dealing with such trauma could easily have avoided the call in the first place or could have retreated at the first sight of true horror of the crash scene. Someone like Teresa could have quit after the first hour, saying enough is enough. But Teresa found herself doing things she did not know she could do, and she kept doing them until the necessary work was over.

I got to know Teresa during that time, and she started visiting with me regularly afterwards. We talked about her family history and background. We talked about what she had been through as a child, as a young adult, and now in her marriage. She opened her history to me and she opened her heart. The trauma of the plane crash triggered memories of past traumas in Teresa. All of the raw-edged and harsh realities of life that confront everyday people that are not easily spoken of during "normal" life get spoken of in times of trauma.

When something like a plane crash makes obvious how much of life is out of our control and how widespread suffering, evil, and sin are in this world, we want to name those broken places in our experience once again. These are parts of life that do not fit the easy surface glibness that the world seems to invite us into. Our common social interactions with those who work with us—and all too often, even those who live with us—do not allow us any occasions to speak out of our broken-heartedness. A large part of our spiritual growth entails being able to survive in a world that both breaks our hearts and hushes us at the same time.

When Teresa was able to speak about her own broken heart, it became clear to her that she had to get out of her marriage. In being able to cope with the trauma that she experienced, Teresa saw a new life opening up in front of her. Her new life was one where she no longer saw herself as a victim or a dumping ground. Her new life was one where she could take some measure of control even in a scene of horror, suffering, and death. This was not the control that could "make it all better," but it was the control to do what she could; it was a self-control. Coming through that, confronting fears, overcoming self-doubts, she caught a glimpse of a life not dominated by shame and fear.

A large part of her new perspective developed in her group Alcoholics Anonymous meetings, but we would also talk together one-on-one for many hours. In those conversations, Teresa often remarked that in Alcoholics Anonymous, she was developing a "spirituality," and yet she also felt the need for something more. This "something more" she was starting to find in church life.

It might seem ironic that someone would develop a conscious spirituality first and a church life second, but that happens more often than we religious professionals would like to admit. What finally is important is not what comes first but that both develop. The mutual support and sharing that small groups can provide is hard to replace anywhere else. But the word of God, the sacraments, and the special way that the Holy Spirit works in the people of the church cannot be replicated in other settings. So Teresa developed both areas. She grew stronger and her self-esteem rose. After a painful struggle with the fact that she could not change her husband nor could she live in the atmosphere of their home, her divorce became final.

About a year later, Teresa met Charlie. Charlie was a farmer in northwest Iowa, and he had never been married. He was a hard-working fellow who taught Country and Western dancing in the evenings for fun. Teresa met him at one of these dance classes, and their relationship grew. Within a year Charlie had asked her to marry him, and she agreed. When Teresa came into my office on the Air Guard base during the next drill weekend, I could tell she was especially happy. She had, in fact, come to tell me about her marriage. She was beaming with real joy, not the giddiness of young-girl infatuation but a strong, deep joy of a mature woman. I celebrated with her when she told me the news. But I was not ready for what she then asked of me.

Following my experience with Susan, I thought perhaps Teresa would ask me to officiate at her wedding. That would have been a great honor as it had been to be a part of Susan's wedding. That is not what she asked me. That morning in my chaplain's office in the Air Guard base, Teresa asked me to give her away at her wedding.

I was so stunned that at first I gave a nervous laugh. She was a little puzzled by my reaction, but I quickly recovered as it started to sink in just what she was asking of me. Her father had died the previous year. I knew that she had been very close to her father and that she was sad he would not be there for the future joys of her life. But I was surprised and humbled by her request to give her away.

Now the very phrase, "giving away the bride" does in many ways belong to a former era, a time when daughters were considered the property of the father to give away or keep as he wished. We have moved away from that older thinking and seek the blessings of families for those marrying. Knowing what Teresa had been through, though,

I knew I would not be giving her away. In thanking her for the honor that she gave to me, I told her that no one could really give her away—except herself. No other person could compel her actions, on that wedding day or any other. She had learned through God's grace that she had been given a life to have and to hold—her own life. She was the one who was in charge of giving it or keeping it. Yet it was important for both of us that I would walk down the aisle with her.

That next April 13, I escorted Teresa Kilburn down the aisle and she left as Teresa Dickmann. In walking down the aisle beside Teresa, I was not "giving her away" but simply walking next to her for a while. That seemed to symbolize our relationship. No, no one can give away someone else. But we can walk with each other for a while. We can listen to others—let them know that they are heard, and they can listen to us and let us know that we are heard. In sharing one with another our histories, our hopes and fears, our hurts, our broken-heartedness, as well as our little victories, somehow God's healing spirit is at work.

These friends come to us as gifts, special friends who walk with us a way, symbolize—no, more than symbolize, *embody*—God's loving presence in our lives. As Teresa was able to move from a life of pain through a traumatic event into a new life, she touched my life by her sharing of who she really is, which is the greatest sharing possible.

Her sharing also allowed me to share who I was, and in the process, grow in my own spiritual walk. We walked down the aisle together as a joyously humble expression of God's calling us into God's future and of God's call for us to walk with one another side by side in the bonds of friendship that only God's spirit can forge.

Not everyone who was involved with the plane crash or any other trauma will find new life in the way that Susan or Teresa did. Not everyone will experience a joyous wedding that symbolizes new life. Human existence is not that symmetrical. But these marriages are, to me, living reminders of the grace of God; they were ritual embodiments of hope. They were truly sacraments, truly events that mediated God's presence. For me, the resurrecting, life-renewing love of God was overwhelmingly present at those two weddings, and it is that renewing love of God that *is* available to all, whether it comes in a wedding or not. Like the resurrection of Jesus Christ, the weddings of Susan and Teresa show that God can bring new life out of even the worst of tragedies.

Some may wonder how I dare speak of hope, new life, weddings, and resurrections even as I write about the horrors of a plane crash. How, after witnessing first-hand the very real suffering and death this life holds for us, can we ever speak with integrity about joy? I understand the question and hope that the questioner will gain a larger perspective on these concerns.

Easy talk of "new life" and "re-creation" can certainly ring hollow in the wrong context or when said in the wrong way. Such talk can be ripe for the ironically—and sarcastically—disposed simply because, like all naked assertions of what is real, it is vulnerable. Sometimes even Christians themselves who, by mouthing simple-minded platitudes about hope and resurrection at the wrong time, only sting the open wounds of true human suffering. By speaking of the resurrection too soon in the grieving process, we can demean its power. By speaking of hope and God's never-ending grace, we do something risky.

To speak of God's grace is risky not only because of the possibility of bad timing but also because in moving from the hard and fast realities of death and suffering to talk about the resurrection and new life, we are moving from the realm accessible through our senses—death and suffering—into a realm accessible only through faith.

This risky move is one that God invites us to make in our everyday lives. Only if we shut our eyes to suffering will resurrection talk ring hollow. Those who know the reality of suffering can most keenly appreciate the fullness of the Good News, and from those who do know suffering, this Good News must not be withheld. We are called in humility to take the risk of speaking the word of hope that has been given to us. We are called in humility to perform the marriage, to walk down the aisle with the bride, to look to the sunrise, to join in the celebrations once again. "I'm alive!"

The weddings of Susan and Teresa came as down payments on, and foretastes of, the final victory that we shall enjoy in Christ. These weddings offered foretastes of the kingdom of God, which shall come fully and finally in God's own time. Until then, we have only occasional, unpredictable—but undeniable—glimpses of hope. Like the Hebrews finding manna in the wilderness, we must receive God's grace wherever we find it, and receive it with thanksgiving. That manna will sustain us until the final wedding takes place, the wedding that scripture promises to us.

*Then I saw a new heaven and a new earth; for the first heaven and the first earth had passed away, and the sea was no more. And I saw the holy city, the new Jerusalem, coming down out of heaven from God, prepared as a bride adorned for her husband. And I heard a loud voice from the throne saying, "See, the home of God is among mortals. He will dwell with them as their God; they will be his peoples, and God himself will be with them; he will wipe every tear from their eyes. Death will be no more; mourning and crying and pain will be no more, for the first things have passed away." And the one who was seated on the throne said, "See, I am making all things new."*

Revelation 21:1-5

## QUESTIONS FOR REFLECTION AND MEDITATION

- Though our lives are filled with sin and brokenness, God also sends signs of hope into the world. What signs can you name in your own life? Begin thinking on as small a scale as you can.

- How can you *cherish* the hope that God has given to us? Without denying the reality of tragedy, actively try to remember the goodness that God has shown to you. Write what you remember in a notebook

- In what ways can the Sunday worship service serve to remind us of the hope God wants us to realize? Consider different parts of the service such as
    – the promises that scripture conveys to us;
    – the hymns and the witness of their composers;
    – the words of the communion liturgy;
    – the words of creeds and confessions.

- How do humility and gentleness allow us to see and receive the signs of hope that God sends into the world?

# THE PRESENCE OF GOD

The reader might think that the hope I spoke about in the last chapter should be the final word on the subject of living after tragedy. But there is something even more important to say about Christian responses to tragedy, and it concerns nothing less than the heart of the whole Christian Gospel.

When I was forced to deal with the reality of a plane crash, not just as something reported in a newspaper article, but as a reality at my very fingertips, I had to live more intentionally. During my ministering after the plane crash, I started living *"in time"* more intensely than I ever had before.

Now, by living "in time" I do not mean "living in the present" the way some pop songs emphasize "living for today" (which, especially in the songs of the '60s and '70s, generally seemed to mean "abandon yourself to your senses, get high, and have sex as much as you can").

No. I have a deeper meaning in mind.

What *does* "living in time" mean? In one sense, this whole book tries to answer that question. But let me try to explain this phrase a little more concisely.

All human beings on earth live "in time," but what I experienced is something beyond that commonplace observation. As someone who had earned four academic degrees and was working as a college professor, I spent most of my time living at the speed of thought, which can be almost as fast as the speed of light. When one lives at the speed of thought, one can leap centuries with a single bound, skim over the pages of human life that dwell on suffering, and bracket-out the confusing diversity that lived life presents to us.

Being thrust into the scene of a plane crash caused me to start living more intentionally, not at the speed of light, but at the speed of *life*. Living at the speed of life means encountering true mystery, true humility, and the over-whelming joy of life-as-gift. It means living where you know that you need healing and forgiveness. The only parallel to the intensity of this life-in-time that I knew after the plane crash was the intensity I experienced when I became a father.

I was in the delivery room when Laura was born, and it was an overwhelmingly powerful and holy time. After the initial rush of awe and joy had swept over me, though, I remember feeling something quite different. A few days after witnessing this birth, I vividly remember standing in my carport in Georgia, weeping with a sense of fear, almost terror.

What was so terrifying to me? Why would the joy of new life bring a sense of fear? After much reflection and prayer, I realized that I had never known anything in my life that had such a hold over me as that new baby. In trying to sort this out, I talked to Denny Groh, a professor of mine from seminary, and he told me something that his fellow professor and our mutual friend Paul Hessert had told him about becoming a father. Denny had known the fear that I spoke about, and that fear had been put into words by Paul Hessert when he told Denny "The world has a hostage now."

That was it for me. The world had a hostage. Certainly my wife had my love, and I had other friendships that were meaningful to me. But that helpless child was a hostage that would change my life. That child would change my life not out of coercion, but simply by being. Maybe, though, being itself carries its own kind of glorious coercion for those who have ears to hear it—the coercion of being, the being that coerces love.

Just by being born, Laura reoriented my life. No longer could I breeze through thinking only of Jody and myself. There was now a wonderful and terrifying grip of love on my heart put there by fathering a child. Two and a half years later, another wonderful "hostage of the world" came into our life; her name is Jenna. Their very being drew me into something mysterious and humbling because it made me aware of how much is so out of my control. Their very being drew me into that life that the plane crash would call me back into—life in time. This life in time is the life of the heart. Living in time at the speed of life means living in your heart, and living out of your heart.


## A RELIGION OF THE HEART

The heart—that metaphor we use to describe the center of who we are, the depth of who we are— is where our emotions are forged. If emotions are anything, they are creatures of time. The dispositions and attitudes that we carry around in us are developed through time. Why is one person fearful and another joyful? Leaving aside genetic, dietary, and hormonal elements, we are who we are emotionally and spiritually because of the history that we have lived in time. It is our heart that carries our history around for us, and it is a "heart religion" that scripture calls us to live.

I am aware that the phrase "heart religion" can conjure a variety of images. For some it can mean a syrupy, smile-at-all-costs celebration of daisies in the meadow on a sunny day. For others, it can mean over-heated revival meetings where every possible aspect of the service focuses attention on the guilt in our lives, to the exclusion of anything else.

These two, quite different, species of "heart religion" have something important in common, though, and that is a valuing of certain aspects of our *real, lived experience.* Different as they are, these examples can each be clearly contrasted with a paper religion that lives only in creeds, and also contrasted with the religion of droll, intellectual cleverness that all too often lives in the seminar and commons rooms of academia. For all of their drawbacks, these two quite different species of "heart religion"—the cheery optimism of the sunny meadow and the guilt and sorrow of a revival meeting—are attractive to some people who want a religion that can be *lived,* enacted, and connected with real experience. People want a religion that can inform, shape, and express their hearts.

In reality, both of my caricatures of heart religion target only part of the overall truth of Christianity. The daisy-filled meadow can indeed lift our spirits and help to reinstall us in the created order. But the plane crashed on a beautiful summer day, under a bright blue sky dotted with puffy little clouds. Nature mysticism does not tell the whole story.

Those aspects of human life that (at least the best of) the revivalists are targeting—the realities of brokenness, evil and sin in our lives—also need to be addressed and

cannot be fully answered in the contemplation of creation. Unfortunately, the truth is—as seen in these examples—that many of us tend to target only a certain part of
our experience and label that one part as the only truly
"religious" experience.

Some people feel that they are being "most religious"
when they experience what they take to be "joy." These
are the people who come most alive at Easter, Christmas,
or Pentecost. Others feel that they are being "truly religious" when they face their own sin and guilt and are
filled with repentance. Lent is the "most religious" season
for them.

The living-in-time heart religion I am talking about,
though, is the heart religion that can be developed only
by experiencing the revelatory aspects of *all* of the seasons
of the church year, and, more importantly, all of the seasons of our lives. The realization of God's presence that
comes at Christmas and Epiphany is meaningful only after
the anticipation of Advent. The joy and release of Easter
is real only after the season of repentance and denial of
Lent. The outpouring of the Pentecost Spirit can come
only from the Crucified and Risen One.

In this sense, the seasons of the church year help us to
live in time at the speed of life. These seasons are formed
by the story of the Bible, and so is the heart religion that
I am talking about. Such a biblical religion has to be lived
to be true; it has to engage the very center of who we are

in the time in which we are planted. It is not one theory among many—even the best of all theories: it is a way of life. The classical creeds and the best theology (religion on paper) can provide only a map of this life. But a map is not the street on which we live.

The heart of the believer as shown in the Bible is both a heart filled with "love, joy, peace" (Gal. 5:22) and a "broken and contrite heart" (Ps. 51:17). The believer's heart must have the capacity for both sorts of experience. More than that, the Bible shows us that the two require each other. The heart that is not contrite cannot know true joy. The heart that has no place for joy, love, and peace is not yet contrite and humble. But to live such a well-rounded and full spiritual life is the challenge of our life on earth. To be able to live fully in all of the seasons of the church year is a demanding task that takes our concentrated effort. I was not always prepared to give that effort.

## BEING SLICK WITH THE WORLD

When I was growing up, even before I had found the ways to avoid living-in-time that academia may afford, I found an easy alternative to experiencing these demanding and sometimes painful movements of the heart. That alternative was to live as a slick and glib practitioner of sarcastic humor.

Laughter is certainly a desirable commodity in this life. When we name those people we call our friends, we are often referring to those who can laugh with us. When men and women are asked to list attributes of the ideal mate, a "good sense of humor" is usually found close to the top of those lists. But laughter can have a darker side and that can be seen in the laughter of mockery and sarcasm.

Making the move from eighth grade into high school was a time of great anxiety for me. Maine Township High School East in Park Ridge, Illinois, was, when I entered it, a school of about four thousand students. It was a bewildering and, at times, a frightening place. I remember spending my freshman year with a tight stomach, walking the halls in fear that I would appear foolish. The world created by that high school environment (and it did seem like a world unto itself) was a world that seemed to hold no place for me. I tried to deal with that world through laughter.

To make that world digestible and to carve out a place for myself in that world, I found things about that world that could be laughed at. I then tried to share those perceptions with my classmates. By the time I was a senior, I had become fairly well practiced in this art, and I was selected as the graduate with "the best sense of humor."

Those of you who remember high school will know that such a designation almost surely suggests that I was quite a smart aleck. This is true. What many high school students value in a sense of humor is slashing, biting, burning remarks that cut to the quick and often express hostility. These remarks "make fun" of situations and people.

Humor, especially sarcastic humor, is abstractive; it de-contextualizes. What is reasonable in one context is outrageous in another, so the humorist takes incidents, swaps contexts, and revels in the ensuing irrationality. ("How did you find your dinner, sir?" the waiter asks. The customer responds, "It was right there on my plate.") This kind of humor is not the kind that promotes harmony, but it did allow me to deal with the world. It allowed me to be "slick."

To be slick with the world was quite an accomplishment. Being filled with fear, uncertainty, and insecurity, and seeing the world as primarily a threat, it was quite an achievement—something to be valued and even cherished—to be slick. To reformulate myself so that none of that world could get to me, so that none of it would stick to me, so that none of me would stick to it, was an achievement that resulted from much effort.

Remembering this personal history of avoiding full-hearted life-in-time through sarcasm, I now wonder how much of that history was idiosyncratic to me and how much is a feature of our whole culture. On virtually every situation comedy on television the biting sting of sarcasm is omnipresent. On the innumerable comedy shows on cable television, and on virtually all the stand-up routines on the late shows, not to mention the movies that appear in the theater, sarcasm is the preferred idiom of our culture. The entertainment industry feeds our hunger for the distancing of strong irony and mockery.

A culture of sarcasm is unsustainable in the long run, however, because of the parasitic nature of sarcasm (and its gentler cousin irony). Sarcasm is a second-order language that feeds off of the first-order assertions of the rest of the world. The thorough-going mocker never asserts anything, for to assert something is to be both real and (something that the mocker is most afraid of) vulnerable. To assert something positive is to open oneself up for the mockery and sarcasm of others. So our culture seduces us into a life of noncommitment—a life of holding back, being "cool," scorning the indicative, saying "no" to living in time.

Being slick with the world—being glib, making the sticky points of life smooth, Teflon-coating our souls so that nothing sticks to them—this is what we are being invited into by our culture of sarcasm. Sooner or later, though, we find that we need something to stick to our souls. We need traction.

The acts of sarcasm and mockery—the process of naming what is worthy of our contempt—though, can help us finally name what we must take seriously. The acid of sarcasm, poured uniformly over everything, finally meets that which it cannot dissolve. The acid of sarcasm finally meets words that cannot be taken—or spoken—lightly.

Throughout my life, I seemed to be asking: What words can I speak with full integrity, knowing that I live in a world of broken hearts? What can I say that I will not relativize through self-deprecation, self-mockery? What can I say that will stand on its own that will express the deepest truths that I know? How can we recover such a speech, such a way of speaking?

This way of speaking both comes out of, and helps to form, a way of living. That way of living is "living in time." Doing ministry in the aftermath of a plane crash, I saw several powerful instances of people living in time and speaking the truth of their hearts. Susan's simple declaration to her dad ("I'm alive") is an example of this. Teresa's question to me ("Will you give me away?") is another. I also caught glimpses of this way of life, and experienced truths which withstood the acid of sarcasm, in music that spoke to me as it had never done before.

Driving to work in the morgue each day after the crash, I would be filled with a tremendous sadness and a heaviness and a desire not to go. I dreaded going, and yet I knew that that is where I was called to be. In the car I found solace and inspiration in listening to an old gospel song, the kind that is easily mocked, the kind that was mocked by my dad. I heard the Forrester Sisters sing

"Love Lifted Me," and tears would come to my eyes, for I knew that, on my way to the morgue love, God's love, was lifting me. I knew that it was not by my own power that I could go and face those realities; I knew God's love was lifting and carrying me into that place.

The simple assertion in that unsophisticated medium of the gospel song had real power. It was this song's very openness to being mocked that made it all the more powerful. It was a naked and defenseless assertion of God's love making a difference in the world, and I knew somehow God used that song to help me live in time at the speed of life.

Another song that invited me to live "in time" was "Enter In," sung by Steve Green. On one level this song is a call to enter into the life "within," that is, to take our experience seriously and pay attention to the movements of our souls. We cannot be content to see and name God only in the Bible or in the stories of past saints. Scripture itself tells us to look for the activity of God in our own lives; therefore we can and must "enter in" to our own experience and name the name of God if the faith of Abraham, Isaac, and Jacob is to be ours too. But the words of this song are also calling for people to "enter in" not only to their own soul, but also into the death of Christ. Only by entering the death of Christ can we know the resurrection of Christ. In this, the song writer is presenting an accurate reflection of scripture, as seen in Romans 6:3-4:

*Do you not know that all of us who have been baptized
into Christ Jesus were baptized into his death?
Therefore we have been buried with him by baptism
into death, so that, just as Christ was raised from the
dead by the glory of the Father, so we too might walk
in newness of life.*

This "entering in" to a life in time though, does not end
at baptism. We see in Luke 9:23-24 another invitation into
the death of Christ, and this invitation is not for a one-time
event, but is a standing invitation into a whole way of life:

*If any want to become my followers, let them deny
themselves and take up their cross daily and follow me.
For those who want to save their life will lose it, and
those who lose their life for my* sake *will save it.*

Only by entering into death daily do we find God's
grace. When we die to our worldly, mocking, slick, sarcastic, self-serving selves, only then can we take on the life
that leads to the kingdom of God.

## GOD IS HERE

I was most powerfully aware of dying to my old way of
life and living in time just a few minutes after I entered
into that crash scene. This event, which was one of the

most transforming events of my ministry, revolves around my speaking some very simple words in the indicative mood of plain assertion. I did not use understatement, overstatement, or sarcasm. I spoke simple words that came from my heart.

When I ran on to that crash site, that runway strewn with the dead and dying, I said something that seems, on the face of it, to be one of the most outrageous and audacious statements a person could make. After I had knelt down and prayed with that passenger named Brad, after I had felt the clammy neck of the dead woman in vain pursuit of her pulse, after I had asked if there were any survivors left in the plane and was pointed to the cockpit, I ran up to the scene near the cockpit. On my way there, I saw the commander of our unit who was running in the other direction to do one of the many tasks that needed to be done. As we were running by each other I caught his eye and made a very flat declarative statement to him, a simple affirmation that has stayed with me in the core of my heart ever since. It was something that I would not have predicted I would say. It was something not tinged with academic hedging or the sarcasm of the seminar room.

When I caught the colonel's eye, I simply looked at him and said, "God is here."

As a theologian, I am fluent in discourse about God. Yet, in my daily life, I have often been hesitant to name the presence of God in everyday reality. I have been uneasy with facile references to "God's will" and more often have remained silent rather than say "God was in situation X" or "God was behind condition Y." I would not risk being wrong. Perhaps my academic "sophistication" led me in the past to be silent about God rather than to be bold. Perhaps my history of worldly sarcasm and cynicism and my fear of being the target of somebody else's sarcasm made me hold my tongue or understate the presence of God. Perhaps it had to do with my commitment to the commandment that we are not to take God's name in vain. Regardless of the explanation for my reticence to speak of God in everyday life, the undeniable truth was that I had never so experienced the presence of God as I did on that runway that afternoon.

I did not say "God is here" with shyness or uncertainty. I did not speak it in the subjunctive mood of wishful thinking. I certainly did not say it in a prideful way, as if God were there because I, a minister, was there. No. I said it because I knew it was true, and I knew I had to say it, and it was something I cannot be sarcastic about. I could not name that truth in a light-hearted way; I cannot now in remembering it, be glib or slick about it. Such an assertion is flat-footed and unsophisticated. It is clearly capable of being mocked. It is in some sense fragile and vulnerable, and yet, in another sense, it is immutable.

God's presence in such a setting is clearly a mystery, but it is a mystery that has a definable shape. Surely in some sense God is everywhere. I heard Douglas Steere say in a lecture at The Academy for Spiritual Formation, "God's breeze is everywhere. We just have to hoist our sails." And it is true that our *awareness* of God's presence does ebb and flow for many different reasons, both spiritual and physical.

But it is also true that God has been revealed in some particular places and times more than others, such as in the history of Israel and the life, teachings, death and resurrection of Jesus. The teachings of Jesus help me understand how the presence of God was so real in the midst of the crash site.

When God was incarnate on the earth in Jesus Christ, the full glory of God was cloaked. To look at Jesus was to see a carpenter with a particular set of parents, a particular hometown, a particular history. Jesus was fully human. But Jesus also promised that in the future, the Son of Man would come again. At this promised coming, the glory of God would no longer be cloaked.

*When the Son of Man comes in his glory, and all the angels with him, he will sit on his throne in heavenly glory. All the nations will be gathered before him, and he will separate the people one from another as a shepherd separates the sheep from the goats. He will put the sheep on his right and the goats on his left.*

Matthew 25:31-33, NIV

This glory-filled coming, though, will not just be about the final judgment. At this awe-filled time, God will also remind us of how God has been present in our world *before* this end time. As Jesus describes the scene,

*Then the King will say to those on his right, "Come, you who are blessed by my Father; take your inheritance, the kingdom prepared for you since the creation of the world. For I was hungry and you gave me something to eat, I was thirsty and you gave me something to drink, I was a stranger and you invited me in, I needed clothes and you clothed me, I was sick and you looked after me, I was in prison and you came to visit me." Then the righteous will answer him, "Lord, when did we see you hungry and feed you, or thirsty and give you something to drink? When did we see you a stranger and invite you in, or needing clothes and clothe you? When did we see you sick or in prison and go to visit you?" The King will reply, "I tell you the truth, whatever you did for one of the least of these brothers of mine, you did for me."*

Matthew 25:34-40, NIV

The God who Jesus revealed to us is here in our midst most unavoidably when we are in the midst of the suffering of this world. We are most acutely aware of God's presence when we can see that all of those who are suffering are our neighbors. We are in the presence of God when we see that the world has us *all* as a hostage. This, I think, is the meaning of love.

On that runway I came to see that the Good News of Christ is not for the slick and glib who never cry the bitter tears of human suffering. No, the Good News is for those who see our risen Lord reaching out for us with his nail-pierced hands in the midst of our broken-heartedness. Not just in our fullness, but most especially in our emptiness, can we see and taste the glory of the King of Kings, the Lord of Lords, the Conqueror of sin and death. It was out of brokenness, it was only after understanding the real corruption and despair of the "world" (to use the Bible's word) that I could more fully pursue the fruit of God's spirit.

To recognize the truth of the gospel, to comprehend the truth of the incarnation of Jesus Christ and the importance of the sufferings of Jesus on the cross, is to see that it is not in the pretended holiness of innocence that we are godly. God instead is present to us—and makes us holy—when we stand in the midst of the wreckage that surrounds us and we name what is real to us. The cross of Jesus tells us that God is here in all that we can go through as human beings. The cross tells us that God is here in our brokenness and pain, in our tears, in our lowliness, in our desolation. The cross of Jesus tells us that God is here.

The empty tomb of Jesus tells us that God will continue to be with us. The Resurrected One invites us into the future with hope. But part of our human failing is that we all too often give away the present in exchange for the future. We think that life is something that cannot be faced, that we must hold our breath through it, so to speak, until we get to the other side where we can finally breathe easily. But that is wrong.

Finally, the most audacious, enlivening, freeing, joy-creating, humbling, and life-transforming reality of the Christian faith is not that God *will be* with us, but that God is *here, right now.* God is here in the midst of suffering, in the midst of joy, in the midst of short-coming, in the midst of triumph, in the midst of our greatest fulfillment, and in the midst of our broken-heartedness. God is here not just at the joy of wedding celebrations. God is here not just in the mourning of memorial services. God is even here in the midst of the crash itself. This is not to say that God *caused* the crash. It is to say that God works in, with, and through our freedom to create possibilities for new life.

As I look back on my recent history, I recognize that I have spent a lot of energy developing dodges for real life, shields against real life, only to have real life—and God—circle back, find me anew, and call me out from behind my shields. From behind the warrior's image of the military uniform, God called me into gentleness.

From the shield of academic distance, God called me to enter in to the life in time. From the shield of sarcasm and mockery, God called me into the simple assertion of God's presence. When I spoke the words "God is here," I found a new vocal range in which to live and move and have my being. That vocal range was available all along, but I was not ready to speak in it until after the crash. I had to be living in time before I could really know the God who entered time.

To name God is the biggest part of my role as a chaplain. It is the biggest part of any ministry. But beyond these professional concerns, to name God is what we as *Christians* are all about. To name the Christian God—and to live in time in the presence of this God of gentle, yet power-filled revelations—is the wonderful call that goes out to *all* believers.

It was in time that Christ died for us, and it is only in time that we can enter into the cleansing power of that death through baptism and a life of spiritual growth. Only when we fully enter into time and live at the speed of life can we find God. Only when we live in the real world that breaks our hearts can we live into the vision of true Christian heart religion.

Because God chose to live in time, then so can we—so *must* we. With all of its contingencies, failures, and shortcomings, time is where God calls us to live. God calls us to enter into this moving stream of life where emotions live. Time is the home of emotions, and emotions are the home where *we* live. Time and the human heart are the arenas of God's presence.

When we choose to enter into this confusing, contradictory welter that is life-in-time, we find a glorious surprise—God is already there! God is there waiting to meet us in all of our humanity! God is already there, joyously working within the self-imposed confines of human freedom to renew us and reshape us back into the image in which we were first created. As it says at the end of the Gospel of Matthew: "And remember, I am with you always, to the end of the age" (Matt. 28:20).

My prayer is that our broken lives and faltering voices will ever shine forth the glorious word that "God is here." This is a word we did not create; it is a word that creates us. This word transposes all of our laughing and crying into the key of God's true and abiding joy. This word does not remove the mystery of tragedy, but it is this word that can start the healing of our broken hearts.

## QUESTIONS FOR REFLECTION AND MEDITATION

- What scares or threatens you about living a "religion of the heart" or what attracts you to it? Are you working on unexamined assumptions about what a heart religion is supposed to be?

- In what ways are you "slick with the world?" How can this be an adaptive feature of your life, and how can it hinder your spiritual growth?

- Many spiritual writers have said that our biggest temptation from God is distraction, being drawn away from the Christian life by the busyness of the world. What are your distractions? How can you be more intentionally aware of God's presence in the midst of your day-to-day activity?

- Sometimes we might fantasize about God appearing to us in a dramatic revelation in the sky, but the scriptures say that God is revealed in other, more ordinary ways. What would you fix your attention on if you were to look for God?

- Consider the different parts of the church year, for example, the seasons of Advent and Christmas, Lent and Easter and the stories each is designed to tell. In which season do you find yourself living your own spiritual life more than others? Reflect on why that is. Is there something about the joy of Christmas or the somberness of Lent that you either fixate on or avoid? Does this have to do with your own personal history? If so, name what it is that prevents you from living more fully in *all* of time the way that God did in the life of Jesus.

- How do you think your spiritual life after a tragedy should be different once you realize that you are living in the presence of God? What concrete steps can you take today to bring your life into conformity with the image of true happiness that Jesus presents to us in the life of a humble, loving, and joyful servant?

- The "means of grace"—those God-appointed ways of opening us up to God's presence—are baptism, communion, prayer (both individual and communal), fasting, searching the scriptures, and being a part of the up-building fellowship of other Christians. Do you use these in your quest to live more consciously in the presence of God? What is preventing you from doing so?